Terms and Conditions

LEGAL NOTICE

The Publisher has strived to be as accurate and complete as possible in the creation of this report, notwithstanding the fact that he does not warrant or represent at any time that the contents within are accurate due to the rapidly changing nature of the Internet.

While all attempts have been made to verify information provided in this publication, the Publisher assumes no responsibility for errors, omissions, or contrary interpretation of the subject matter herein. Any perceived slights of specific persons, peoples, or organizations are unintentional.

In practical advice books, like anything else in life, there are no guarantees of income made. Readers are cautioned to reply on their own judgment about their individual circumstances to act accordingly.

This book is not intended for use as a source of legal, business, accounting or financial advice. All readers are advised to seek services of competent professionals in legal, business, accounting and finance fields.

You are encouraged to print this book for easy reading.

Table Of Contents

Forward

Chapter 1:
The Basics

Chapter 2:
You Must Grow

Chapter 3:
Keep Part Of It

Chapter 4:
Proclamations

Chapter 5:
What Is Your Financial Future

Chapter 6:
Verbal Training

Chapter 7:
Learning

Wrapping Up

Foreword

This book deals with the personal successes of everyone us. Success means achievements as the result of our own efforts and abilities. Proper planning is the key to our success. Our acts may be no wiser than our ideas.

Our thought may be no wiser than our understanding. The objective of all life is developing; and everything that lives has an unalienable right to all the development it's capable of attaining.

Babylon became the most affluent city of the ancient world, as its citizens were the richest individuals of their time. They treasured the value of money. They applied sound financial precepts in gaining money, maintaining money and making their money pull in more money. They supplied for themselves what we all want...monies for the future.

Becoming The Richest Man In Post Modern Babylon

Collections Of Money Related Wisdom Gathered From Timeless Principles And Parables.

Chapter 1:
The Basics

Synopsis

In the annuls of history there was no city more glamorous than Babylon. It's very name arouses visions of riches and magnificence. Its treasures of gold and gems were fabulous.

Babylon is a great example of man's power to accomplish great objectives, utilizing whatever means are at his disposal. As a city, Babylon exists no longer.

Nowadays, this valley, once a thickly settled irrigated farming district, is once again a wind-swept arid waste. But it's inhabitants weren't mere barbarians living inside protecting walls.

They were an educated and knowledgeable people. The glory of Babylon has faded however; its wiseness has been preserved for us.

Behind It All

Whatever might be stated in praise of impoverishment, the fact remains that it is not possible to live a truly consummate or successful life unless one is wealthy. No man may rise to his greatest height in talent or growth unless he has plenty of income; for he must have a lot of resources to use, and he can't have these resources unless he has net worth to purchase them.

A man grows in mind, soul, and body by making use of resources, and society is so organized that man has to have money in order to become the owner of things; consequently, the basis of all forward motion for man must be the skill of getting wealthy in all areas of life.

The city of Babylon was coordinated much like a modern city. There were streets and shops. Peddlers provided their merchandise through residential areas. The Babylonians were skilled in the arts. The Babylonians were also clever financiers and traders. As far as we know, they were the original inventors of money as a means of exchange, of notes and written titles to material possessions.

In a few hundred years, it was in time abandoned, deserted, left for the winds and storms to level again to that desert earth from which its splendor had originally been built. Babylon had fallen, never to develop again, but to it, civilization owes a great deal. The wisdom of Babylon endures.

- Money is the thing by which earthly success is assessed.
- Money makes possible the enjoyment of the best the earth provides.
- Money is plentiful for those who comprehend the simple laws, which govern its attainment.
- Money is regulated today by the same laws today as long ago.

Man's right to life means his right to have the free and non-sensitive use of all the things which might be necessary to his best mental, spiritual, and physical unfolding; or, put differently, his right to be wealthy.

No man should be satisfied with a little if he's capable of utilizing and enjoying more. The purpose of life is the advancement and unfolding of it; and each man ought to have all that can bestow to the power; elegance, beauty, and richness of life; to be content with less is iniquitous.

The man who possesses all he wants for the living of all the life he's capable of living is rich; and no man who hasn't plenty of money may have all he wants. Life has become so complex, that even the most average man or woman needs a great amount of wealth in order to live in a fashion that even comes near completeness. Each individual naturally wishes to become all that they're capable of becoming; this want to realize innate possibilities is built-in in human nature; we can't help wanting to be all that we may be.

There's nothing wrong in needing to get rich. The want for riches is truly the desire for a richer, fuller, and more abundant life; and that want is praiseworthy. The man who doesn't desire to live more abundantly is abnormal, and so the man who doesn't want to have money enough to purchase all he wants is abnormal.

There are 3 motives for which we live; we live for the body, we live for the brain, we live for the soul.

Not one of these is better or holier than the other; all are desirable, and not one of the three--body, brain, or soul-- may live fully if either of the others is cut short of total expression. Man can't live fully in body without beneficial food, comfortable clothing, and warm shelter; and without freedom from undue labor. Rest and recreation are likewise necessary to his physical life.

He can't live fully in brain without books and time to study them, without a chance for travel and observation, or without intellectual company.

To live fully in soul, man has to have love; and love is denied expression by impoverishment.

A man's highest happiness is discovered in the bestowal of advantages on those he loves; love finds its most natural and spontaneous expression in giving. The man who has nothing to provide can't fill his place in the world. It's in the use of material resources that a man finds full life for his body, develops his brain, and unfolds his soul.

It's consequently of supreme importance to him that he should be rich.

It's perfectly right that you ought to desire to be rich; if you are a normal man or woman you can't help doing so.

Chapter 2:

You Must Grow

Synopsis

A chariot master of Babylon was thoroughly disheartened. From his seat on the low wall fencing his property, he gazed unhappily at his simple house and the open shop in which stood a partly finished chariot.

Develop

His wife often appeared at the open door. Her sneaky peeks in his direction reminded him that the food cupboard was nearly empty and he ought to be at work finishing up the chariot, so he could collect from his rich buyer.

Even so, his fat, muscular body sat stolidly on the wall. His slow brain was fighting patiently with an issue for which he could discover no answer.

Beyond his home loomed the high terraced wall encircling the king's palace. . In the shadow of such grandeur was his simple house and many others far less fancy. Babylon was like this—a mixed bag of grandeur and squalor.

He chanced upon his best friend—a musician. "Might the Gods bless thee with great liberalness, my good friend," started his friend. "Yet, it does look as if they've already done so as thou needest not to work. I rejoice with thee in thy good luck.

The chariot master replied, I'd even share it with thee if I had more. The musician replied, thy purse which must be bulging else thou wouldst be engaged in your shop, pull out but two small shekels and lend them to me till after the noblemen's feast this night. Thou wilt not miss them before they're returned."

"If I did have two shekels," the chariot master responded gloomily, "to no one may I lend them—not even to you, my best friend; for they would be my fortune—my whole fortune. No one lends his whole fortune, not even to his best friend."

"What," exclaimed the musician, "Thou hast not one shekel in thy purse, yet sit like a statue on a wall! Why not finish that chariot? Have the Gods brought to thee pains?"

"A torment from the Gods it has to be," he agreed. "It started with a dream, in which I thought I was a rich man. "A pleasant dream, indeed," remarked the musician, "but why ought such pleasant feelings as it aroused turn thee into a gloomy statue on the wall?"

"Why, indeed! As when I awoke and recalled how empty my purse was, a feeling of revolt overcame me. What is the matter? Why can't we acquire silver and gold—more than enough for food and robes?

At last, I recognize this will never do. Therefore, my heart is sad. I wish to be a rich man.

But how mayest thou secure it while we both of us are as poor as the king's slaves asked the musician? We don't wish to go on year after year living slavish lives. Working, working, working! Getting nowhere."

"May we not discover how others acquire gold and do as they do?" the chariot master inquired.

"Perhaps there's some secret we may ascertain if we but sought from those who experienced.

"Thou bringest to me a rare thought", said the musician. "It costs nothing to ask wise advice from a great friend. No matter though our purses are as hollow as can be. Let that not detain us.

We're weary of being without gold in the middle of plenty. We wish to become rich men. Come; let us go to ask how we, also, may gain incomes for ourselves."

Thou makest me to see the reason why we have never encountered any measure of wealth, state the chariot master. We never sought it.

Now, ultimately, we see a light, bright like that from the rising sun. It biddeth us to learn more that we might prosper more. With a fresh understanding we shall find honorable ways to achieve our desires."

Chapter 3:
Keep Part Of It

Synopsis

In old Babylon, there once lived a certain very wealthy man named Arkad. Far and wide, he was famed for his great wealth. Too was be famed for his liberalness.

He was generous in his charities. He was generous with his loved ones. He was liberal in his own expenses.

But even so, every year his wealth increased more quickly than he spent it.

His take on money went like this: "If you have not acquired more than a bare existence, it's because you either have failed to learn the laws that govern the building of riches, or else you don't observe them. He found the road to wealth when he decided that a part of all I earned was his to keep. And so will you.

Put Some Back

Riches come from the development of assets (hard currency, stocks, property, or any additional asset). Assets are bought with revenue. If you don't put aside part of your revenue to gain assets, you'll discover it extremely tough to acquire wealth. All the same, if you do put aside part of your income to develop assets, you'll find it really easy to acquire wealth. It's all very easy.

You can't invest what you don't have. So the opening move is to, guess what, save some revenue! Not once, but systematically and consistently. But consider it like this:

Let's make up an easy example for instance. Let's say one week is compiled of ten days. And let's suppose you work for all those ten days. You earn $100 every day. This is week 1. By the finish of week one, you've pulled in $1,000. Now, if you spend the whole thousand and you've none of it left by week two, your whole efforts for week 1 have vaporized! You've nothing left to show for your endeavors. Zip! What were you working for?

You gave away all your revenue. You paid everybody else except yourself! Now, here is something you ought to realize: No successful or wealthy person does that! None!

And if you're doing it, then it should not be a surprise that you aren't amassing riches. So how ought you live if you wish to begin amassing riches? Well, let us continue with our illustration. In week 1, you'd keep 10% of your revenue, and spend the remaining revenue you earn and you'd do the same each week.

Regardless what, you'd keep that contract with yourself, the contract to pay yourself first. It's honoring you, respecting yourself. It's a testament that you believe that you have a future meriting investing.

It's a testament that you value your work, your revenue, what you bring in for yourself. You don't pay everybody else and persist with nothing! Why in the world would you do that when it's your revenue!

You merit keeping part of it; after all, it's you who brought it in. So, even in week 300, you'd still have with you the 10% from week 1, and every additional week.

And you wouldn't keep this revenue so you will be able to spend it on a vacation, car or something like that (that ought to come out of your other percentage). You keep it so that it put up work for you, bear babies for you, and make you more of its own. You worked for it, and now it's time to have it work for you. So, you invest it right from the outset.

And as you're re-investing your returns (the babies the money bears), your investment will be intensifying itself, so the babies themselves will be bearing babies of their own, into many generations. The gains you brought in week 1 will be re-invested and they'll bring in more money themselves in week 2 and so forth, and that revenue itself will earn more revenue in week 3 and so forth... And this simply grows into what you call riches, generations on generations of your revenue earning for you.

And it all begins when you respect yourself enough to ensure that regardless what occurs, you preserve at least 10% of what you earn each week! You pay yourself first.

Set up your life so that, regardless what, regardless what, you keep at least 10% of your income each week. And don't spend and hope some will be remaining to save and invest. Pay yourself first of all, first, prior to the bills, the gas, the food, the apparel, the ... Pay yourself first of all.

Chapter 4:

Proclamations

Synopsis

The utilization of favorable statements like daily affirmations may draw in wealth and create an admiration for all life's thrills. During these times of over-the-top change and sacrifice, everybody may benefit from a continuous flow of revenue through multiple sources. We shall talk about the power of wealth statements, which may alter your life now.

Say It

Money is whatsoever you decide it to be. Money may be currency or a thought. You were produced in the image of the creator. The root of the word creator is create. That means you are able to create and you have originative faculties – the mental power to bring into your life whatsoever you want.

Be clear about the sum of money you wish to take in. State it and signify it. Think about all the things you wish to act with money. Bear a great love for income, and visualize money coming to you in as many dissimilar avenues as you are able to imagine. Envision yourself spending all the revenue you want, as if you already have it.

Let each action, tone, and display of character be from the mentality of being rich now. Consider this – you're requesting and you merit an abundance of revenue to be used to increase the lives of those you love and humanity. In you acquiring what you want today, you ought to be abundantly overjoyed and thankful. Maintain the attitude of gratitude and be thankful for everything you have, so you'll get more of it. Replace words of deficiency like, "I don't have enough", or "I can't afford that". Quit compelling yourself to receive less and begin compelling yourself to get increase, abundance, prosperity, riches and wellness.

Here are a few daily affirmations to draw in wealth and all the good you want and deserve into your life today:

* I'm constantly furnished with what I require.
* Life is simple, and I have an abundance of what I require.
* I now have excess, and all my needs are getting met.
* I have limitless abundance.
* I now give freely and get freely.
* This world is limitless, and there's plenty for all of us.
* Income comes to me easily and often.

Be thankful for the money you have. Make a list of all the things you'd purchase with an abundance of money. Treasure all the riches around you and the riches of other people. Treasure the wealth of goodness and love present in nature and inside you. Maintain a firm faith that income is coming.

Ask yourself frequently, am I attracting income now or blocking it with my ideas? Remember to constantly pay yourself first before you pay your creditors. You're telling the forces of the universe that you're worthy and worth more.

Affirm, "I'm so happy and thankful now that income comes to me in increasing amounts through multiple sources on an uninterrupted basis." Say it frequently throughout the day. Do whatever it takes to feel great today. The emotions of delight, faith and gratitude are mighty money magnets. So be as happy today as you would be with all the income you want. Always sustain favorable statements in your mind.

Making daily affirmations apart of your life may draw in wealth and keep you centered on appreciating all the good that is inherent in all things. Wealthiness is a mentality. You attract what you think of. Ask the best. Think only of the best. You shall become the best and consequently get the best. It's all about what you believe."

Chapter 5:

What Is Your Financial Future

Synopsis

Ascribable to the present state of our economy, there are a lot of individuals losing their jobs, discovering overtime being cut at their jobs and not acquiring pay raises in order to stay up with inflation. By nature, individuals question themselves on how to control their financial future in this afflicted economy. In the accompanying steps below, I'll show you some practical ways on how you are able to get control of your financial future.

What's You Can Do

Cut back on your life-style –

Ascertain what you're spending your revenue on and see which expenditures are crucial to you and which ones are simply draining your monthly budget. There are a lot of things that you are able to cut back on that won't have a great impact on your overall quality of life, like eating out less frequently, have more family suppers at home, take a coffee mug to work and keep away from buying a $4 cup of coffee, carpool with your colleagues that live in your area, bag your lunch, take the public transportation system to work, and so forth.

Establish an emergency monetary fund -

You ought to plan ahead and build your emergency monetary fund gradually in order to sustain greater control over your financial future and not simply before a major money crisis. Maybe, if you take the essential steps now, perhaps you could utilize some of the savings from the above step in order to lend to building your emergency monetary fund. It's suggested to have at least six months of your living disbursements in your cash reserves.

Broaden your sources of revenue -

Do not simply rely on your day job for all of your money needs. There are a lot of opportunities that you are able to capitalize on in your spare time. For instance, beginning a part time home based business, build up your investment portfolio; turn over buying residential real property to rent out or cashing in on your spare-time activity.

"The life of each man proceedeth from his childhood to his old age. This is the path of life and no man might deviate from it unless the Gods call him prematurely to the world on the far side. Therefore do I say that it behooves a man to make preparation for a desirable income in the days to come, when he's no longer young, and to make provisions for his family should he be no longer with them to comfort and support them.

This lesson shall instruct thee in supplying a full purse when time has made thee less able to learn." So said the rich friend of the chariot master.

"The man who, as of his understanding of the laws of wealth, acquireth a growing surplus, ought to give thought to those future days. He ought to plan sure investments or provision that might endure safely for many years, yet will be available when the time arrives which he has so wisely expected. "There are various ways by which a man might supply with safety for his future.
He might provide a hiding place and there bury a secret treasure. Yet, no matter with what skill it be hidden, it might nevertheless become the loot of thieves. For this rationality, I advocate not this plan.

"A man might buy houses or lands for this purpose."A man might loan a small sum to the moneylender and increase it at regular periods.

"But as we live in our own day and not in the days which are to come, must we make the best of those means and ways of achieving our purposes. Therefore do I advocate to all men, that they, by wise and well thought out techniques, do provide against a lean purse in their mature years. Provide in advance for the needs of thy growing age and the protection of thy family."

Chapter 6:
Verbal Training

Synopsis

What were you schooled about money as you were growing up? Something like "income doesn't grow on trees", or "money is the root of all evilness", or maybe "all rich individuals are greedy"?

Well, how do you expect to get to be a success financially if you trust these things? You draw in into your life what are thinking of and what you trust. If you think there is not enough income in this world for everybody you'll never have adequate money.

What You Think

First off, believing that "revenue doesn't grow on trees" is an illustration of what's called lack or scarceness programming. Our parents schooled us that there was never enough income to go around, and that it wasn't readily available or abundant.

But really, the universe is really abundant, and there's lots of income to go around for everybody. Just think what you could do if you have so much revenue to fill all your heart desires. What marvelous things you could do with it: travel to the countries you've always dreamt of, purchase a house you even scared to toy with it, attend meditation classes so you may spiritually grow, donate revenue to your favorite charity, spend more select time with your loved ones and the list goes on.

The key is to begin thinking that you deserve the revenue and that there's lots of it available for you, and then you are able to begin attracting it into your life. That's abundance thinking, which is the inverse of lack or scarceness thinking.

Once you begin thinking of the abundance, the Law of Attraction will accomplish the rest. You don't need to know how it is going to occur simply make the first step, beginning thought. Beginning is already winning.

And what about thinking that "revenue is the root of all evilness"? Can you truly expect to become a success if you trust that money is the root of all evilness?

Unless you have a want to be an evil individual, your subconscious mind will not let you have income if you trust deep down that it's the root of all evilness.

Now that you comprehend that, you are able to begin to think that money is as a matter of fact good; you're able to help people with money. You are able to stimulate the economy with revenue. Even the most kind-hearted spiritual individual, who says they don't need money, may do more to make the world a better place with revenue than without it.

And what about thinking that "all rich individuals are greedy"? Well, that produces us versus them, whereby you've labeled all of "them" greedy in your brain. You, on the other hand, are very giving in your brain. That's why you don't have revenue, because you're not greedy.

Sure, there must be a few rich individuals in the world who are greedy. But there are likewise poor individuals who are greedy. There are both rich and poor individuals who are very giving as well.

The sum of money you have has nothing to do with these persona traits.

As a matter of fact, a lot of rich individuals got there by not being greedy. Having a giving mental attitude opens up a flow of revenue that often brings them more. You'll discover the same thing... give away revenue joyfully to an acquaintance, and notice that it comes back to you in another form.

The world needs to be a balance of reciprocation, and being joyful both as you give and get will ensure that you always go with the flow.

And altering your mind-set from what you were taught as a youngster to a healthier view of income will allow you to become the financial success you merit, to become true you.

Chapter 7:
Learning

Synopsis

"This day do I speak to thee, my pupils, of one of the most critical remedies for a lean purse. Yet, I will talk not of gold but of yourselves, of the men neath the robes of many colors who do sit before me.

I'll talk to you of those matters inside the minds and lives of men which do work for or against their success." So did the rich man of Babylon address his class.

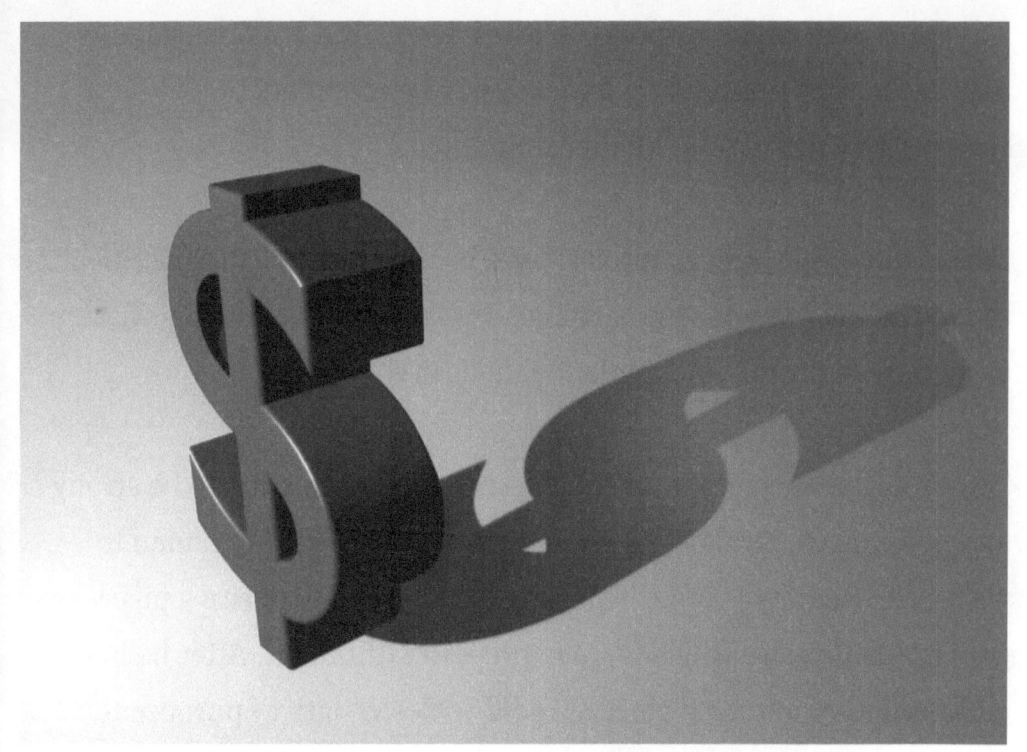

.What Are You Following

"Not long ago came to me a beau seeking to borrow. When I interrogated him, he sounded off that his earnings were deficient to pay his expenses. With that, I explained to him, this being the case, he was a pitiful customer for the moneylender, as he owned no surplus earning capability to repay the loan.

"What you require, young man,' I told him, 'is to take in more coins. What dost thou to step-up thy capacity to earn?'

"All that I may do' he responded.'Six times within 2 moons have I approached my master to call for my pay be modified, but without success. No man may go oftener than that."

"We might smile at his simplicity, yet he did have one of the critical requirements to better his earnings. Inside him was a strong want to earn more, a proper and applaudable desire.

"Preceding achievement must be desire. Thy desires has to be strong and definite. General wants are but weak yearnings. For a man to wish to be wealthy is of little purpose. For a man to desire 5 pieces of gold is a real desire which he may press to fulfillment. After he has endorsed his want for 5 pieces of gold with strength of purpose to assure it, next he may find similar ways to get 10 pieces and then 20 pieces and later a 1000 pieces and, behold, he's become wealthy. In learning to secure his one definite little want, he hath trained himself to secure a bigger one. This is the operation by which wealth is amassed: first in small totals, then in larger ones as a man learns and gets more capable.

"Wants must be simple and definite. They kill their own purpose should they be too numerous, too confusing, or beyond a man's training to achieve." As a man perfecteth himself in his calling even so doth his power to earn better. In those days when I was a lowly scribe carving on the clay for a few coppers every day, I observed that other workers did more than I and were compensated more.

Consequently, did I determine that I would be surpassed by none. Nor did it take long for me to distinguish the reason for their greater success. More interest in my work, more immersion upon my task, more doggedness in my effort, and, behold, few men may carve more tablets in a day than I. With fair promptness, my increased skill was honored, nor was it necessary for me to go 6 times to my master to call for recognition.

"The more of wisdom we recognize, the more we might earn. That man who seeks to learn more of his craftsmanship shall be richly honored. If he's an artisan, he might seek to learn the techniques and the tools of those most adept in the same line.

If he laboreth at the law or at curing, he might consult and exchange knowledge with other people of his calling. If he were a merchandiser, he might continually seek better goods that may be bought at lower prices.

"Always do the matters of man change and better because keen-minded men seek keener skill that they might better serve those upon whose patronage they depend. Therefore, I advocate all men to be in the front rank of progress and not to stand still, lest they be left. "A lot of things come to make a man's life rich with gainful experiences. Such matters as the following, a man must do if he value himself:

- "He has to pay his debts with all the punctuality inside his power, not purchasing that for which he's unable to pay.

- "He has to take care of his loved ones that they might think and speak well of him.
- "He has to make a will of record that, in case the Gods call him, suitable and honorable division of his property be achieved.
- "He has to have compassion on those who are injured and smitten by misfortune and aid them within fair limits. He must do deeds of thoughtfulness to those dear to him.

"Thus this remedy for a lean purse is to cultivate thy own powers, to study and become wiser, to become more skillful, to so act as to Regard thyself. Thereby shalt thou develop confidence in thy self to accomplish thy carefully considered desires."

Wrapping Up

A lot of individuals will scoff at the thought that there's a way of getting rich; holding the impression that the supply of wealth is fixed, they'll insist that social and governmental institutions must be altered before even any considerable number of individuals may acquire a competence.

But this isn't true. It's true that existing mindsets keep the masses in poverty, but this is as the masses don't think and act in the sure way.

www.ingramcontent.com/pod-product-compliance
Lightning Source LLC
Chambersburg PA
CBHW030551220526
45463CB00007B/3059

If the masses start to move forward as advised in this book, nothing may check them.

If the individuals have the advancing brain, have the trust that they may become rich, and move forward with the fixed aim to become rich, nothing may possibly keep them in poverty.